DR CHRISTIAN'S

GUIDE TO

YOU

Dr Christian Jessen

Illustrated by
David Semple

SCHOLASTIC

With thanks to Anita Ganeri for her brilliant research
and invaluable help.

Scholastic Children's Books,
Euston House, 24 Eversholt Street,
London NW1 1DB, UK

A division of Scholastic Ltd
London ~ New York ~ Toronto ~ Sydney ~ Auckland
Mexico City ~ New Delhi ~ Hong Kong

First published in the UK by Scholastic Ltd, 2016

ISBN 978 1407 16544 8

Printed and bound by Tien Wah Press Pte. Ltd, Malaysia

2 4 6 8 10 9 7 5 3 1

CONTENTS

DR CHRISTIAN

HELLO

keeping fit

I'm so pleased to have a chance to tell you about some really important stuff that will help make you fit, healthy and wise! This book is a guide FOR you and TO you – a blueprint for a happy and healthy future. Hopefully it should help you set yourself up for success in every part of your life.

Talking to adults about personal stuff can be hard and it often seems like they don't really understand you and your problems. The aim of this book is to help you feel more confident about what is going on in your life, and more confident about talking about these sorts of issues. If your mum or dad seems particularly confused then send them to their room with this book and tell them not to come out until they have read it! Parents often need help too and my aim is that this book will be just as useful for them as I know it will be for you.

After you have read it you can go out into the world and be brilliant, change history and make your mark. And if that all sound a bit too much for now, then start by simply being kind to other people, especially those who may not be as confident or happy as you. And if they are having trouble with any of the issues in this book, then you will be just the right person to help them. And maybe, if you feel you have learned everything inside it, you can pass the book on to them.

Dr Christian

HEALTHY EATING

During puberty, your body starts changing from a child's body into an adult's. There are changes on the outside and inside, both physical and emotional. Because you're growing up so fast, you burn up loads of energy, and probably feel hungry a lot of the time. A balanced diet is essential to help you stay at a healthy weight, and look and feel your best.

But is it really as easy as that? Our busy lifestyles can be hard on our health. It's tempting to dash back from school and grab an unhealthy snack, or skip breakfast so you can spend an extra half an hour in bed, but it's not a great idea. To keep your growing body in top condition, you need to eat a diet rich in fruit and vegetables, as well as nutrients such as iron and calcium. This way, you'll be able to cope better with all the changes that are happening to you and get into good food habits that will last you for the whole of your life.

FACT FLASH

You might find that your taste buds are changing, too, and you start liking food you'd never have touched before. It's a good time to experiment with different things to eat and discover things that you like and that are good for you.

BALANCED DIET

Eating a balanced diet is very important for staying healthy. 'Balanced' means eating a variety of different foods that give you all the energy and nutrients you need. The food plate below shows you the proportions of each type of food you should eat. Try to get the balance right over a day or even over a week. You don't need to do it at every meal.

VEGETABLES, FRUIT
These can be fresh, frozen or tinned. They're packed with essential vitamins and minerals which your body needs to stay healthy. You should try to eat as much of these as possible.

BREAD, RICE, POTATOES, PASTA
Starchy foods like these are called carbohydrates (or 'carbs') and give you energy.

MILK, CHEESE, DAIRY FOODS

These contain protein, which helps you grow, and calcium, which keeps your growing bones and teeth healthy and strong.

MEAT, FISH, EGGS, BEANS

Another important source of protein, vitamins and minerals, which your body needs to grow and stay healthy.

FATTY OR SUGARY FOODS

Foods such as biscuits, cakes, chips and sugary drinks that you should only eat in small quantities, as treats.

The labels on packets of food will tell you if something is high in fat, salt and sugar, but all the numbers can be tricky to understand. Some labels use a simpler traffic-light system – red, amber and green. Red means high, amber means medium and green means low. Foods that have more greens on the label are the healthiest choice.

FACT FLASH

Despite what you may have read online or in magazines, fat IS important and you certainly do need some in your diet. But too much of the WRONG fat is bad, especially if it's saturated fat. This is found in foods such as cheese, cakes, sausages and butter. Try to cut down how much saturated fat you eat and choose foods that contain unsaturated fat instead, such as oily fish, vegetable oil and avocados.

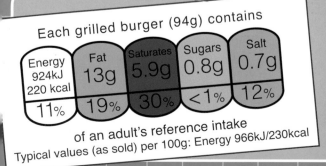

Each grilled burger (94g) contains

Energy 924kJ 220 kcal	Fat 13g	Saturates 5.9g	Sugars 0.8g	Salt 0.7g
11%	19%	30%	<1%	12%

of an adult's reference intake
Typical values (as sold) per 100g: Energy 966kJ/230kcal

Sticking to the general guidelines shown on these labels is a good way of ensuring we are eating as well as we can. But you shouldn't get too bogged down with the numbers. Remember that everyone is different, and what is right for one person may not be right for someone else.

TOP HEALTHY EATING TIPS

There is a lot of advice around about which foods are good for you and which foods aren't, and it can get very confusing. The best thing is to eat a wide range of different foods to make sure that you're getting a balanced diet and you don't get bored or feel you're missing out. Here are some top tips for getting your healthy eating habits off the ground.

STARCHY FOODS, such as bread, pasta and potatoes, should make up about a third of your food. Choose wholegrain varieties when you can – they've got loads of fibre and help fill you up. And eat jacket potatoes with the skin on – it's the best bit!

EAT AT LEAST FIVE PORTIONS OF FRUIT AND VEG A DAY. It's easier than it sounds. A glass of (unsweetened) fruit juice counts as a portion, or you could sprinkle some chopped banana or apple onto your cereal at breakfast.

EAT MORE FISH – it's packed with protein, vitamins and minerals. Try to eat at least two portions a week, including oily fish, such as salmon, fresh tuna and trout. Oily fish is good for keeping your heart healthy and makes sure your brain is working well too – important for exams!

CUT DOWN ON SUGAR, especially when it's added to fizzy drinks, cakes, biscuits and breakfast cereals. Swap sugary cereals for porridge, and fizzy drinks for water, squash with no added sugar or semi-skimmed milk.

CUT DOWN ON SALT. Eating too much salt can be bad for you, but sometimes you might not even realize you're eating it. Even if you don't sprinkle salt on your food, there's lots of it already added to foods such as ready meals, breakfast cereals and bread.

BOOST YOUR IRON. This is especially important for girls, who lose iron when they have their period. Plenty of foods are rich in iron, including red meat, pork, poultry, seafood, dark green vegetables (spinach, watercress), beans (chickpeas, red kidney beans) and wholegrains (wholemeal bread). Iron helps build muscles and healthy blood cells.

Ask Dr Christian

Help! I'm hungry all the time.

Q. I feel hungry all the time. I'm always starving by morning break and when I get home from school I eat loads of toast or cereal to keep me going until dinner. I don't seem to put on any weight, though I've grown loads this year. My mum says I'm eating her out of house and home! Is there something wrong with me?

A. It sounds like everything is perfectly okay to me and you are exactly how I was at your age! Teenagers eat - a lot! And it's perfectly normal. My mother called me a locust, eating her out of house and home. You are at an age when physical, emotional and hormonal changes come at an enormously fast rate. So you have high energy requirements, which can make you feel hungry all the time. Growth spurts also increase your requirement for food. Of course it is possible that you have some bad habits, like skipping breakfast because you got up too late, or consuming a lot of foods containing artificial sweeteners. These may make you feel more hungry because they trick your body into thinking that sugar is on the way. Insulin is released to help store it, but when the expected sugar never arrives, your blood sugar levels drop, making you feel hungry.

Ask Dr Christian

How much should I eat?

Q. I'm confused about what is a normal portion of food. In my family we always have really big servings and Mum says you have to finish what's on your plate even if you're not hungry. Sometimes I feel absolutely stuffed after dinner. Is that normal?

A. I would hate to disagree with your mother (because as you will know well by now, mothers are always right!) but I think that always finishing your plate, especially if it is a large portion, can lead to bad habits and weight problems. There is a lovely and clever rule that I often tell people: eat until you are no longer hungry, not until you are full. Think about it, there is a difference. We are all different – we are different sizes, do different things – and so we all have different energy requirements. Guidelines say that teenagers need around 2,000 calories a day, but obviously this won't be the same for everyone. If you are putting on too much weight, then you are eating too much. It's simple.

HEALTHY SCHOOL LUNCHES

You're sitting in class, and your tummy starts to rumble. You're starving! At last, the bell rings and you can head down to the cafeteria for lunch. School dinners used to have a bad reputation but they've come a long way since then (well, most of them!). Schools are trying hard to provide appetizing, healthy meals for their students, but it's still up to you to make the right choices when you get to the front of the queue.

Particularly when you get to secondary school, you have a lot of control over what you eat for lunch. There is more choice, for starters, and you are also expected to be more responsible – you won't have someone checking that you've eaten your vegetables or drunk your water. You've left that behind at primary school. With all this choice and freedom, it can be tempting to go for a less healthy option, especially if you're really hungry. And it's fine to go for pizza once a week so long as it isn't every day! Try to remember the advice about eating a balanced diet over the whole week. Apart from all the other benefits, it will give you the energy to get through your afternoon lessons.

Here's an example of a good, balanced school lunch:

Tuna pasta bake, carrots, peas, fruit, water

PACKED LUNCH?

You might prefer to take a packed lunch to school. Then you can choose exactly what you want to eat. Of course, a packed lunch isn't necessarily healthier than one you buy at school – it all depends on what you put in it. All of the rules about healthy eating apply! Make sure you talk to your parents about what you want to eat so that they can stock up. You could also offer to make your own lunches – it's a great way to show that you're growing up.

Here's an example of a good, balanced packed lunch:

Chicken wrap, carrot sticks, tomatoes, slice of malt loaf, fruit, water

TOP TIP
Whether you're taking a packed lunch or buying a school lunch, try not to eat the same things every day. Eating a mixture of different foods will help you stick to a balanced diet, and stop your taste buds from getting bored.

SMART SNACKING

Do you get straight home from school and raid the cupboard for snacks? Do you find yourself constantly grazing on food? Again, we are all different and different eating habits suit different people. Because I work out in the gym a lot I can't get by on three meals a day. I prefer to have five smaller meals so I don't have to go so long between eating. I suggest that you aim for three regular meals a day and two snacks. Having a snack isn't necessarily unhealthy, but it depends on what you're snacking on. It's tempting to grab something quick like a bar of chocolate or a bag of crisps and that's okay occasionally. But most of the time try to stick to healthy snacks – it's just as easy to munch on an apple as to wolf down a piece of cake and it'll fill you up for longer. Get your parents to help by stocking up on healthy snacks at home.

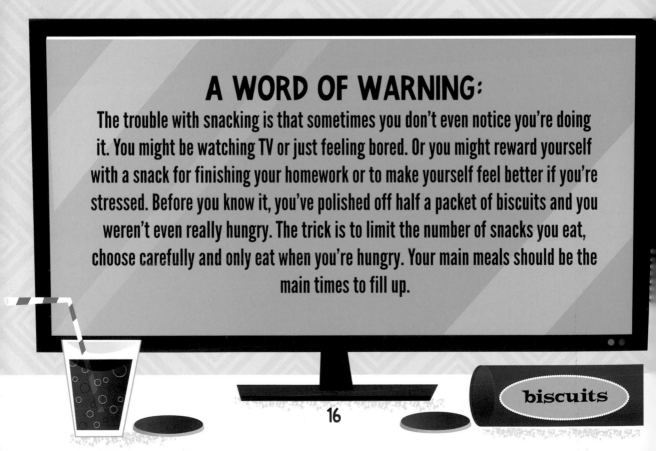

A WORD OF WARNING:

The trouble with snacking is that sometimes you don't even notice you're doing it. You might be watching TV or just feeling bored. Or you might reward yourself with a snack for finishing your homework or to make yourself feel better if you're stressed. Before you know it, you've polished off half a packet of biscuits and you weren't even really hungry. The trick is to limit the number of snacks you eat, choose carefully and only eat when you're hungry. Your main meals should be the main times to fill up.

biscuits

SUPER SNACKS

• Chunks of fruit – for example, apples, pineapple, pears, tangerines, kiwis, strawberries, melon, grapes – or a banana (easy to eat on the go!)

• Dried fruit – for example, apricots, banana, mango

• 'Trail mix' – a mixture of raisins, sultanas, pumpkin seeds, sunflower seeds and dried cranberries

• Crumpet, rice cakes, oatcakes, pitta bread or bagel with houmous/cottage cheese/peanut butter*

• Chopped-up veg – for example, carrots, peppers, celery, cucumber, cherry tomatoes

• Yoghurt

• Plain popcorn

• Unsalted nuts*

• Boiled eggs

* Unless allergic. And if you're offering snacks to a friend, remember to check if they're allergic to nuts too. Some schools won't let you have nuts as part of a packed lunch, but at home it's fine.

Ask Dr Christian

Is it okay to skip breakfast?

Q. I don't usually eat breakfast in the morning. I'd rather have 15 minutes extra in bed and I don't feel that hungry first thing. I usually just have a snack at morning break, or wait until lunch. My parents think it's bad for me, but I don't see why.

A. Okay, so here is a confession. I used to do this. Teenagers are not good at getting up in the mornings and I used to stay in bed until the last possible second. This meant I nearly always missed breakfast but was, of course, starving hungry by 11am. So hungry I couldn't concentrate or work well. You can see that this isn't good for a school day. So, even if you hate getting up and prefer to sleep in a bit longer, make sure you take some food with you to eat on the way. You really will be grateful for it.

Ask Dr Christian

Why do I eat more when I'm feeling down?

Q. I always crave unhealthy food if I'm feeling sad. After a bad day at school I just want to curl up on the sofa with a packet of biscuits. How can I get out of this habit?

A. It is very, very common to eat more when you are feeling sad about stuff. It is called emotional eating. The problem with it is that it doesn't help with whatever has got you down, and it can lead to really unhealthy behaviours when it comes to food. I recommend that when you find yourself wandering over to the snack cupboard because you have had a bad day, you ask yourself two questions: How am I feeling? What do I need? If you are feeling down, then you are probably not feeling hungry and so what you need is not food, but someone or something to cheer you up. Instead of eating, phone a friend, go and play with the dog or go into town for a bit. Try it – it really works. How am I feeling? What do I need?

FAST FOOD?

How often do you eat fast food? Every day? Once a week? Once a month? What's your favourite – BURGERS, FRIED CHICKEN or CHINESE TAKEAWAY? Fast food's called 'fast' for a reason – it's quick and easy to grab on the go. The downside is that it's often packed with fat, sugar and salt, which are unhealthy if you eat too much. So, it's fine to have a burger as a treat – just as long as you don't do it too often.

Fresh food?

As well as fast food and takeaways, ready meals that you heat up in a microwave are also very popular. Again, they're quick and easy to prepare but they're often full of sugar and salt… and they don't always taste as nice as the picture on the box would lead you to suppose! The healthiest way to prepare food is to cook it from scratch, using fresh ingredients. Ask your parents to show you how to make some simple but nourishing meals, such as pasta with tomato sauce or tuna; chicken and salad wrap; or scrambled eggs on toast. They don't take long – you just need to do a bit of planning ahead to make sure you've got the ingredients on standby. Stock up on basics, such as pasta, rice, tuna, vegetables and salad, and you'll always have something that you can put together in a hurry.

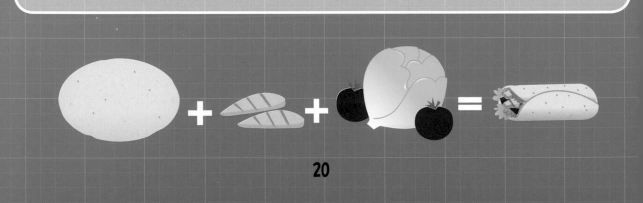

Ask Dr Christian

Is fast food really bad for me?

Q. I've heard it doesn't matter what you eat, just so long as you don't eat too much. Is that true?

A. I suppose this is sort of true in parts, but you do need to make sure that you are getting the balance of different food groups right. When I talk to my patients about food I never, ever tell them to stop eating something altogether (however unhealthy), especially if they really love it. I do tell them to cut down on it and introduce more variety to their diet. So if you are only eating junk food, there is no way you will be getting all the food groups in the right amounts. You can have some fast food occasionally, but just not all the time!

The jury is still out on whether fast food is really addictive, but at the end of the day it is still really all about portion size. That said, fast food is designed to taste really good and to make you want more, so is often high in sugar and fat – and therefore high in calories. It also tends to have a lot of added salt, again to enhance the taste. More and more fast food restaurants are providing nutritional information on their menus, so if you do decide to have some now and again – which is fine – make sure you aren't going for the high fat, high sugar and high salt options as it will take you a very long time to burn off all the calories in it!

WHAT'S TO DRINK?

To stay healthy, your body needs water – otherwise it can't work properly. When your body doesn't get enough water, you can become dehydrated and you'll start to feel ill. If in doubt, check your pee. Normally it's a pale-yellow colour, but if you're dehydrated, it'll be dark and strong-smelling.

GOOD DRINKS' GUIDE

• Water is the best thirst-quencher so make sure you know where the water fountain is at school, or keep a water bottle handy.

• You don't just get water from drinking water though. Squash, tea and even soup are all good sources of fluid. And lots of foods, like fruit and vegetables, contain water, too.

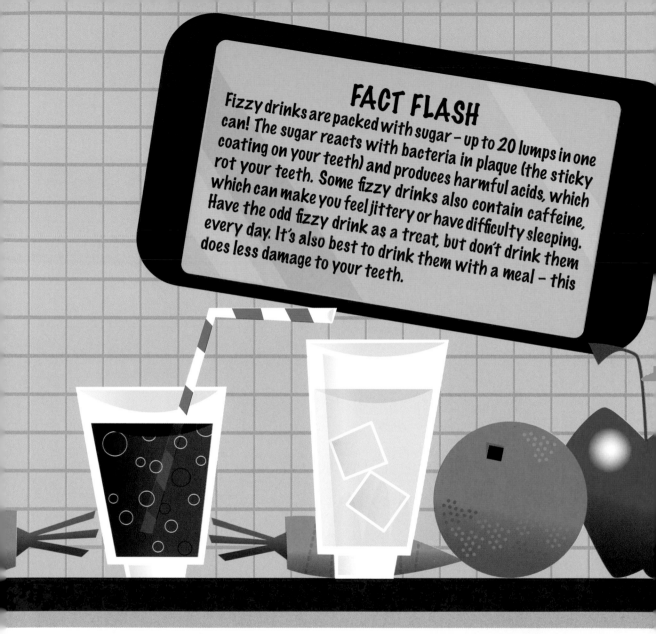

FACT FLASH

Fizzy drinks are packed with sugar – up to 20 lumps in one can! The sugar reacts with bacteria in plaque (the sticky coating on your teeth) and produces harmful acids, which rot your teeth. Some fizzy drinks also contain caffeine, which can make you feel jittery or have difficulty sleeping. Have the odd fizzy drink as a treat, but don't drink them every day. It's also best to drink them with a meal – this does less damage to your teeth.

• Just drink when you're thirsty. Drink a bit more if the weather's warm or if you've been doing exercise.

• Milk is also good for you and a great source of calcium, which is good for strong teeth and bones. Go for semi-skimmed milk.

• Fruit juice can be refreshing, but often contains lots of sugar so limit how much you drink. Too much can rot your teeth so water it down, or reduce your intake to maybe a glass in the morning and a smoothie later on.

GET ACTIVE!

Staying healthy is not just about eating a balanced diet. Getting active and keeping fit is very important, too. Regular exercise every day will help to keep your body healthy, make your bones and muscles strong, and keep your heart and lungs working well. It will also help you to stay at a healthy weight. What's more, exercise makes you feel better by releasing hormones that make you feel happy and relaxed.

Again, it can be difficult to fit exercise into a busy lifestyle. When you've rushed back from school feeling totally exhausted it can be tempting to collapse in front of the TV and stay there. The trick is to find something you enjoy. That way, you're more likely to want to do it and to want to keep doing it over a longer time. There are lots of suggestions on pages 30 and 31. Getting started can be difficult, especially if you're not naturally sporty. But as you begin see results, and to look and feel better, you'll find it much easier to keep going and enjoy it.

SCHOOL

TOP TIP

If you make exercise part of your life, you'll find it easier to stick at it. Get into the habit of doing some exercise every day. It doesn't have to be anything complicated – going out for a walk is a brilliant way of keeping fit.

EXERCISE IS GOOD FOR YOU!

It's official! Exercise is good for you – here are some of the reasons why:

It helps to keep your body at a healthy weight.

It keeps your bones and muscles healthy and strong.

It lowers your risk of certain diseases, such as diabetes and high blood pressure.

It keeps your heart and lungs in good working order.

It helps you have fun and make new friends.

It boosts your self esteem and makes you feel more confident.

It produces chemicals called endorphins in your brain. These make you feel happy.

It lowers stress and makes you feel more relaxed.

It improves your memory and concentration and helps you do better at school.

It teaches you teamwork and other useful life skills.

It helps to boost your immune system so you catch fewer illnesses, like colds.

It gets more oxygen to your skin, which helps to improve your complexion.

Ask Dr Christian

What if I'm not sporty?

Q. I've never been good at PE and I never get picked for any teams at school. I would like to do more exercise, but I don't know what I could do. I'd be embarrassed if anyone saw me because they know I'm not sporty at all.

A. So here's the thing: I'm not sporty. I hated sports at school. Well, when I say that I should say that I hated team sports. I quite liked stuff I could do on my own and was not overly competitive, like swimming. I found team sports to be pretty humiliating and unpleasant, especially as I wasn't very good at them and really couldn't see the point. I do not for one moment think that *everyone* should have to do team sports to help them work better in groups and be better, more well-rounded adults. Self esteem comes from feeling good about who you are, so I suggest you try to find things that you do like to do and see if you can do these instead.

GETTING STARTED

So, you know that keeping fit is good for you but how do you get started? There's no one best way to exercise – try lots of different things out and see what you like. It's really important that you enjoy it, so if you hate running, don't run – find something else. There are loads of things you can do to get moving, you just need to find what suits you best. Remember, this doesn't mean suddenly turning into a football ace or a skateboarding whizz. There are plenty of simpler ways of getting exercise into your day.

TOP TIPS FOR GETTING STARTED

1. Don't put it off. Start today by going out for a walk.

2. Walk or bike to school or a friend's house instead of going by car (remember to ask your parents first).

3. Mow the lawn, hoover your room or wash the car – it's all exercise PLUS you'll get mega brownie points from your parents.

4. Walk around the playground at break instead of sitting or standing around.

5. Put some music on and dance to your favourite tunes.

6. Try to vary the things you do every day so you don't get bored.

FACT FLASH

For all-round fitness, you need to combine exercises for stamina (the ability to keep doing an activity without getting tired), suppleness and strength. This means mixing aerobic exercises (that get your heart beating faster and quicken your breathing), with strength and flexibility training. Some sports, such as swimming, gymnastics and football are good for all three, or you could add some stretches and push-ups to your favourite exercise.

TOP TIP

When you're starting any new exercise, begin slowly and gradually build up to avoid getting injured. It's normal to ache a bit after you've been working out, but if anything really hurts or you have difficulty breathing, stop immediately and get it seen to.

SPORTS TO TRY

There are so many sports and activities out there, it can be difficult to pick which one to try first. To keep yourself motivated, try a good variety, both team sports and ones you can do by yourself. If you don't like the idea of going to a class or a gym, for example, why not get a few friends together and set up your own circuit in the garden or in the park? It doesn't matter what you do, as long as it's fun and gets you moving. Here are some ideas:

Tennis

Netball

Basketball

Walking

Dancing

Hockey

Running/jogging

Football

Dodgeball

Swimming

Gymnastics

Pilates

Rock climbing

Horse-riding

Yoga

Badminton

Martial arts

Skateboarding

Trampolining

Scooting

Rugby

Cycling

BMXing

Ice skating

Volleyball

Golf

Fencing

Archery

TOP TIP

If you're going to the gym, make sure you get a qualified instructor to put together a suitable workout for you, or join an exercise class. It's good to mix some cardio work with weight-bearing exercises for your muscles and bones, and some stretching.

HOW MUCH EXERCISE?

Experts recommend that you aim for at least an hour of exercise a day. On days when you have PE at school, this isn't going to be a problem but on other days, it can sound like a lot to fit in. Don't worry. The good news is that the hour can include walking to school, walking between classes, taking part in activities and sports at school, even playing frisbee in the park with the dog. Better still, you don't have to do it all in one go. You can divide it into shorter bursts of say, 15 minutes, throughout the day.

Your workout should include 'moderate' and 'vigorous' activities. Moderate activities are things like playground games, cycling and riding a scooter. They should make you feel warmer, breathe harder and your heart beat faster, but you should still be able to talk.

VIGOROUS ACTIVITIES

MODERATE ACTIVITIES

Vigorous activities are things like running, swimming and football. They should make you feel warmer, breathe much harder and your heart beat more quickly so that it is difficult to talk without taking a breath. On three days a week, you should also include some exercises for strengthening your muscles and bones, such as push-ups, running and jumping.

FITNESS BUDDY

Ask Dr Christian

I feel too self-conscious to do sport.

Q. I want to start doing more sport and I think I'd like to go to the gym because I prefer exercising alone. But everyone at the gym looks so intimidating! I don't want to wear tight leggings and I don't have fancy trainers. I feel so out of place and like everyone is staring at me.

A. Tight leggings? Let me tell you that you will never catch me in tight leggings! I wear what I feel most comfortable in and I work out all the better for it. And you should see my trainers! They look like something the dog likes to chew... Everything can feel intimidating before you start. Standing up in class to read or speak, going on stage, playing an instrument in front of people. But in the gym you are not really having to do anything for anyone else. You are there for you, and you alone. And if some of the other people there look really toned or have big muscles then remember this, they had to start somewhere, and that somewhere is exactly where you are now.

Ask Dr Christian

Am I doing too much exercise?

Q. Is it true that you can do too much sport? I do sport every day, and I feel really anxious if something gets in the way of my exercise.

A. It certainly is true. Exercising can become an unhealthy obsession rather than a healthy pastime and I would suggest that if you get stressed when you are not able to exercise then you are getting dangerously close to the unhealthy side of sport. I used to worry a lot when filming and work got in the way of working out, but then I reminded myself that rest days are just as important as exercise days. Your body needs time to grow, recover and repair and one night in between exercising simply isn't enough. I suggest you make sure that you have two days off each week to give your body a chance to sort itself out. You will then find that your performance improves too.

SWITCH IT OFF!

How much time do you spend on your smartphone or tablet, watching TV or playing computer games? Do you get straight home from school and immediately start texting or messaging your friends? With so many electronic gadgets at your fingertips, it's tempting to spend a lot of your time glued to a screen, big or small. Screen time is important, for doing your homework and having fun. But too much screen time, combined with too long spent sitting still, is really bad for your health.

Try to limit the amount of time you spend in front of a screen – no more than two hours a days is ideal – and get physically active instead. That way, you'll get your exercise and won't be tempted to snack on unhealthy foods. Before you plonk yourself down in front of the TV, stop to think – could you do something more active instead? And make sure that you turn your phone and tablet off at night. Then you won't be tempted to keep waking up and checking that you haven't missed anything.

Ask Dr Christian

Help! I'm always on my phone.

Q. My parents are always bugging me to put my phone away, but whenever I do I miss out on so much stuff! Everyone else will be online chatting and posting things together. If I'm not there, I'll just be left out.

A. I hear what you are saying about not wanting to miss out on what your friends are doing online. I worry about that too sometimes. But if you think about it, isn't there someone, somewhere, posting something online every second of every minute of every hour of every day? That's quite a lot to be trying to keep up with. And if you think about it a bit more, aren't you missing out on so much other stuff when you are on your phone too? It's all about balance – giving time to your friends, to your family and to yourself. It's really important that you give your brain a chance to rest and go outside and do some exercise. If you find that you have problems getting to sleep then it may be your phone that is to blame. Try rationing yourself to an agreed amount of time per day and see if you can stick to it. It's difficult isn't it? But that shows how much we have become slaves to technology. I don't know about you but I don't want to be a slave to anyone or anything.

SLEEPY HEAD

Growing up can be exhausting! Apart from being busy keeping fit, there's school, seeing friends, doing homework and going to clubs or sports practice. By the end of the day, your body is ready for a well-earned break and a chance to recharge for the next day – and this is where a good night's sleep comes in.

But what's the point of sleeping – why is it so important? Let's see what happens if you don't get enough sleep:

You have trouble thinking clearly

You're unable to do simple tasks

Your body doesn't grow as much (you grow more when you're asleep)

Complex tasks require more effort

Your body is less able to fight disease

Your memory isn't good

Healing slows down (most healing takes place when you're asleep)

So it's pretty important to get enough sleep, especially if you have an important test or exam the next day.

FACT FLASH

If you're aged between 5-12, you should probably have at least 9.5 hours of sleep at night, and as much as 10-11 hours. Teenagers need around 8.5-9 hours' sleep, but some people need more sleep than others and that's perfectly normal.

Ask Dr Christian

Mum thinks I'm lazy but I'm always tired.

Q. I find it really hard to get out of bed in the mornings, and on weekends I'll often sleep until 10 or 11am. My mum says that I'm really lazy, but I just feel so tired all the time.

A. You are definitely not really lazy. You are completely and utterly normal for your age. Teens need their sleep. You probably find that you are able to stay up late at night and find it hard to get to sleep, and also find it equally hard to get up in the mornings. This is because the hormones that your brain produces to regulate your sleep are set to a different cycle from those of younger children and adults. Your sleep hormone - melatonin - only starts to be produced by your brain at around 1am, whereas an adult is producing theirs around 10pm-ish so they are ready for bed well before you. Teenagers also need much more sleep than adults because it is during sleep that various hormones involved in growth are released and do their job. Catching up on sleep at the weekend is good and I suggest you do it. If your mum doesn't believe you, then stick this paragraph under her nose and I'll tell her myself!

BODY CLOCK BLUES

The trouble is that having a lie-in at the weekend can have the opposite effect, and disrupt your body clock even further. You may still find yourself suffering from lack of sleep, even though you've spent the whole morning in bed.

Not getting enough sleep can cause lots of problems (see page 38). So, if you're not going to sleep until late at night, but still having to get up early for school, you could be finding it tough to stay awake during the day. Luckily there are some things you can do to get your body clock ticking again. Here are a few to get you started:

• Don't shout at your mum if she comes into your bedroom in the morning and opens the curtains and turns your light on. It may seem cruel, and the last thing you need, but the light will actually help to wake your body clock up.

• If you feel sleepy during the day, try to stay awake! Distract yourself by doing something active, like going for a walk or having a kick-about, even if you don't feel up to it. It will stop you dropping off and keep your body clock on track.

• If you are planning on catching up on your sleep at weekends, try to go to bed earlier, rather than sleeping in until lunchtime. That way, you'll get your extra sleep in without sending your body clock into a spin.

I CAN'T SLEEP!

Some teenagers have the opposite problem – they find it difficult to get to sleep. Lack of sleep can make you feel terrible and affect how well you concentrate and perform during the day. There are many reasons why you might be having trouble sleeping, such as a change in your routine – moving house or school, or being ill – but there's plenty you can do about it.

TOP TIPS FOR A GOOD NIGHT'S SLEEP

1. Be active during the day. Exercise is also a brilliant de-stresser and makes you feel more relaxed. Don't work out just before bed, though, or it'll make you feel more awake.

2. Try to go to bed at the same time every night. This helps your body get into a good sleeping routine. As part of your routine, have a warm bath or hot drink (that doesn't contain caffeine), or read for a while, to make you relax.

3. Use your bedroom for sleeping only. Make it a tech-free zone for at least an hour before you go to bed. Watching TV in bed, going on Instagram or waiting for a text to ping through can make it hard to fall asleep. This is because the blue light emitted by your devices stimulates certain areas of the brain, keeping it alert and making it harder to doze off.

4. Make your bedroom as relaxing and comfortable as possible. Is your bed crammed full of toys, with no room for you? Are you too hot or too cold at night?

5. If none of these things work, try not to lie awake worrying. This will make things worse. The more you stress out about not sleeping, the less likely it is that you'll fall asleep. Counting sheep or counting backwards from 100 can help to take your mind off things.

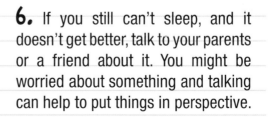

6. If you still can't sleep, and it doesn't get better, talk to your parents or a friend about it. You might be worried about something and talking can help to put things in perspective.

BODY IMAGE

What do you see when you look in the mirror? Are you happy with the way you look? If you aren't, don't worry – you are not alone. Most people are unhappy with some part of their bodies, and have bits that they'd like to change. You might think that you're too short, or too tall, or wish that you had straighter or curlier hair. There's often pressure from your peers or from the media or social media to look a particular way. Whilst it is definitely important to be fit and healthy, sometimes this pressure can make you feel really down, and can get a bit out of control.

JUST ME
magazine

How you see yourself is called your body image, and many people, both girls and boys, have a very negative one. It's quite natural to care about how you look to some extent but if it's making you feel miserable or unhappy about yourself, or you're spending too long thinking about it, this is a BAD THING. Everyone is and looks different, and it's really important to try to accept yourself as you are. After all, you are brilliant because of who you are and what you do – not because you look like a celebrity or not.

TOP TIP

One way to feel better about yourself, especially as your body is changing, is to work on good posture, and walk tall even it makes you feel self-conscious. You'll look more confident, even if you're not feeling it!

CHANGING SHAPE

During puberty, you may feel more self-conscious because your body is changing so much. GIRLS get taller and their bodies start to fill out. Your hips get wider and rounder, your breasts grow bigger and you probably put on some weight. BOYS also get taller and heavier. Your chest and shoulders get broader, and your upper body gets more muscular. Your new body can take a bit of getting used to, but it is perfectly normal and nothing to be worried about or ashamed of. Remember, though, that everyone develops differently and at different times and that can be tough. Don't worry if you're growing at a different rate to your friends. You might feel out of step now, but eventually everything will balance out and you, or they, will catch up.

SCHOOL PHOTO

GROWING UP

As you hit puberty, you may find that your jeans are suddenly way too short, or the sleeves on your favourite top don't fit. Then there's people telling you how much you've grown. This is called a growth spurt. Between the ages of around 12–13, you'll probably grow faster than at any other time in your life, and this spurt can last for two to three years. The fastest-growing bits are usually your arms and legs. This can feel pretty weird, at first, until the rest of you catches up. While this is happening and you're getting used to your new shape it's perfectly normal to feel a bit clumsy – this is because your brain simply can't keep up. You should have finished growing by around the time that you're 15. By the time that you're 18, you'll be at your adult height.

FACT FLASH

While you're growing, you might get some strange aches and pains, especially in your legs. They're sometimes called 'growing pains', although experts don't know if they are actually linked to growth spurts. They usually don't need special treatment and will go away on their own.

BODY IMAGE AND SELF-ESTEEM

During puberty, your body is changing fast, and, with it, your image of yourself. Having a positive body image means being pretty happy with the way you look most of the time. But some people find it hard to look in the mirror and like everything they see. Sadly, this leads many teenagers to have a negative body image and to spend too much time thinking or worrying about their looks, and how they can change them.

The trouble is that a negative body image can be closely linked to feelings of insecurity and low self-esteem. Self-esteem is all about how much you feel that you are worth, and how much you feel that other people value you. It is important because it can affect how you think and behave. If you have a positive body image, you probably like and accept yourself for who you are. You feel comfortable and confident, and this helps to boost your self-esteem. Negative body image can lead to you feeling unhappy about yourself and your life. It can make it difficult to feel confident enough to make friends and to try out new things.

Six steps to better body image

1. Be proud of your body for what it is and the amazing things it can do.

2. Make a list of things you like about yourself that have nothing to do with looks. Read it often.

3. See yourself as a whole person — don't just focus on things you don't like in the mirror.

4. Surround yourself with positive people who like you just the way you are.

5. Block out any negative thoughts telling you that you don't look good enough. Focus on positive thoughts.

6. Rememember — there are things about you that you can't change. Accept them.

Ask Dr Christian

I hate my body!

Q. My friends are all really skinny and pretty, but even if I don't eat more than them I still have massive hips and big thighs. I don't know if I'll ever learn to be happy with the way I look.

A. Very often we can put too much emphasis on what others think about us, or what we think they think about us. Sometimes there can be lots of focus on outward appearance, making us forget that who we are on the inside is equally, if not more important.

It sounds like you know you should accept yourself but right now it's difficult for you, because you keep comparing yourself to others. But your friends actually come in all different shapes and sizes, and I bet they have just as many doubts about themselves as you do. You might think your friend has lovely hair, but they may very well hate it! We are all different and being different is not a negative thing. However, when we doubt ourselves it can change the way we view things, making us see only the similarities that others have and not the differences.

Ask Dr Christian

I look really fat in the mirror.

Q. In my head I know that I'm not overweight, but that doesn't match what I see in the mirror. What I see is that I'm really fat and need to lose weight. My friends and family tell me I'm not, but I just don't see what they see.

A. Worrying about being overweight when you aren't is not uncommon, but suggests that you may have anxiety and self-esteem issues that are making you think this way. It is really important that you listen to people you trust, and if they tell you that you really are not fat then you must try to accept this. Skipping meals or restricting your food to try to control your weight (especially when there is no need) can lead to serious health problems and I would really like you to tell someone if you have been doing this. There are specially trained people who can help you sort out the way you feel about yourself. Please ask for help if you feel you need it - you are never alone with your problems.

BODY PRESSURE

It's not just your own body image that you have to cope with. Today, there's huge pressure from the media and social media to look a certain way. With apps such as Instagram, Facebook and Snapchat, photos can be posted everywhere instantly – there's no hiding place. This can lead to problems when people, including friends, start to comment on what they see. Negative comments can be very upsetting, but positive comments can also make you feel uncomfortable or bad about yourself if you don't look a particular way.

The media, especially the TV and magazines, is also full of pictures of 'beautiful' people with seemingly perfect bodies. But remember, these photos are not always what they seem. In real life, most of these celebs don't naturally look like this. They have had help with their clothes, make-up and hair, and the photos have almost always been 'doctored' or photoshopped by computer to get rid of any imperfections.

LOOK AT ME

...after

before...

Ask Dr Christian

I don't know how to deal with online comments.

Q. At school there's so much pressure to spend ages perfecting photos to put online for everyone to rate and make comments on. It's so fake though! It's like everyone's afraid to show their real selves because they might not look perfect and people might make nasty comments. I don't want to join in, but then I would get totally left out.

A. I wonder if you realize just how intelligent you are to be able to look at the latest craze with a critical eye, see right through it and identify the problems. You are quite right in your assessment of the way some people use social media. Many people can be very hurt by comments left about their photos. It is a form of bullying.

If you don't want to take part in it then don't. If you really feel left out then you could adapt things until they make you feel more comfortable – make a rule that you never enhance any photos you post, or decide that you will never leave a nasty or negative comment about someone. Other people may see how much nicer this is and might start doing it too. And before you know it you will have started a new trend!

WHAT'S THE RIGHT WEIGHT FOR ME?

It's very common for girls, and some boys, to worry about their weight. You might hear friends complaining that they feel fat, even though they're a perfectly normal, healthy size. One problem is that TV shows and magazines are full of pictures showing people who are very thin but this doesn't mean that's the right weight for you.

Being very overweight is not healthy for you, and can cause problems later on in your life. But it can also be unhealthy to be too thin, especially if you are skipping meals or eating less food than your body needs. The best weight for you is the one that is right for your body type and build. Eating well and staying active are the best ways to stay at a healthy weight. But, like your height and hair colour, your genes (the physical features passed down by your parents) have a lot to say about what weight you'll be. Some people eat loads and are skinny; others are naturally stockier, but both may be the right weight for them.

FACT FLASH

During puberty, your body has to build up some fat as an energy store to cope with all the changes you're going through. This may make you put on a bit of weight but it's quite normal and not bad for you.

54

Ask Dr Christian

I'm worried about my weight.

Q. I mainly watch TV or play computer games after school, so I don't do much exercise. I've put on quite a bit of weight this year, and a few people at school have made nasty comments but my mum says I look fine. How do I know if I'm overweight?

A. If you have any concerns about your weight then I suggest that you have a chat with a school nurse or doctor, or even your GP. They will be able to advise you if your weight is okay and be able to tell you the sorts of things you could try doing if you wanted to get your weight under control. One thing I can tell you now: skipping meals is definitely not the answer. The solution is just about increasing the amount of exercise you are getting whilst making sure you are eating a wide variety of foods, not too much junk and sweets, and plenty of fruit and veg. It doesn't need to be any more complicated than that.

DIET DILEMMA

The word 'diet' just means the collection of food that you eat regularly – and a balanced diet is a good variety and mixture of foods. But people often say that they're going on a diet when they want to lose some weight. This means that they cut down on the amount of food they eat and the number of calories they are taking in. We measure how much energy there is in food and drink using units called calories. If you eat fewer calories than your body uses up, you may lose weight.

Maybe you think you should be on a diet? The answer is: you shouldn't be! This sort of diet is bad news when you're growing up. Your body needs a good supply of healthy, nourishing food to help it develop properly, especially during puberty. Being picky about the sorts and amount of food you eat can also lead to having problems with food in later life.

Some diets don't include a good range of foods, drastically cut calories or cut out some groups of foods altogether. These are called fad diets, and they usually promise quick weight loss. Magazines are full of celebrities who have supposedly lost weight this way. The trouble is that these sorts of diets often have nasty side effects (and once you stop the diet, the weight often goes straight back on!). Cutting out carbs (carbohydrates), for example, can leave you with bad breath, constipation (not being able to go for a poo) and feeling tired – hardly the best way to feel good about yourself.

Food should be enjoyed and is a big part of socializing with friends and family. Controlling your food so that you're often hungry or feel ill is never a good idea. The only diet you need to be on is a healthy, balanced diet teamed with plenty of exercise!

DO DIETS WORK?

I can't think of a single celebrity-endorsed diet, or 'latest craze' diet that actually works in the long term. Many of them can result in people putting even more weight on after! In short, diets don't work. At your age you should be getting a good balance of everything in what you eat, and that includes carbs, fats and proteins. Let me tell you why some of the more popular celebrity fad diets are not worth your time or efforts:

WHEAT-FREE DIET

The claim is that we are all getting fatter, and we are all eating much more wheat, therefore wheat is making us fat. The truth is that we are all eating much much more of everything. Eat no wheat at all and you will still get fat if you overeat. Some people do have an allergy to a part of wheat that can cause bad tummy problems, but a doctor will diagnose this after specific tests have been done.

ALKALINE DIET

The theory is that 'acidic foods' make us sluggish, destroy our bones and make us prone to disease. And that adhering to alkaline diet-approved foods will make the body alkaline and more healthy. This is such a load of nonsense that I don't know where to begin! The pH (acid/alkaline balance) of our blood is regulated by our kidneys and diet doesn't change the pH for any significant length of time. That's aside from the fact that the strong acid in our stomach that we use to break down our food will quickly stop any 'alkaline' food being alkaline for long!

RAW FOOD DIET

This diet claims to cleanse you of toxins caused by cooking which, according to the theory, destroys key nutrients and important enzymes that make your body healthier. Rubbish. Your liver and kidneys do a superb job at removing toxins from your body. A raw carrot will make no difference whatsoever. And some nutrients, like the lycopene in tomatoes, can be more completely absorbed into the body if they are cooked, especially if they are cooked with some kind of fat. So now you see why I go on about variety!

SUPERFOODS

Sorry, there is no such thing as a superfood. All fruit and vegetables have their individual benefits and in combination these benefits are enhanced. No one food will make you particularly healthy over and above another.

JUICE CLEANSE DIETS

Juice diets claim to help you lose weight and rid your body of toxins. They supposedly give you more nutrients than eating whole fruits. The truth? There is no evidence that making something into a juice allows you to get more nutrients out of it. In fact, there are some real problems with consuming only juice. Fruits are full of sugar, so people on juice cleanses can consume too much sugar without noticing, and the lack of fibre in a juice diet can cause digestive problems. Long term, these diets can cause hair loss and skin problems too – I've seen patients really suffering because they've been on juice diets.

Overall, being aware of how much fat, sugar, processed food and refined carbohydrates you eat, and how bad these things are for your health when eaten to excess, is good. Getting overly fanatical about it and restricting your diet back to a minimum is not. There is no diet that can magically give you limitless energy or fix your brain. And that's good news, not bad. Because it means eating healthily doesn't have to be boring or hard work or expensive and anyone can do it.

EATING DISORDERS

Some people become so worried about their weight that they start to have serious problems around food. They feel sure that life would be better or they would be more popular if they were thinner, and they start restricting what they eat or obsessing over everything they eat and every bit of exercise. Sometimes they do it as a way of trying to take control of their lives when things are tough in other areas. If these problems get out of control, they take over their lives, making them seriously ill and desperately unhappy. This is called an eating disorder. Eating disorders can affect anyone – girls and boys, as well as adults. There are three main types:

ANOREXIA NERVOSA

Sufferers are so afraid of putting on weight that they keep cutting down the amount they eat until they are literally starving. Even when they get extremely thin, they still see themselves as fat and continue to eat as little as possible. Side effects include weak bones, hair loss, brittle nails and downy hair on the arms and neck. Without help, they may die.

BULIMIA NERVOSA

People with bulimia 'binge' (eat lots of food, fast and in one go), then make themselves sick or take laxatives (medicines that make you go for a poo), to stop them putting on weight. Then they start all over again. This can cause serious damage to their digestive systems, their teeth may start to rot and their eyesight can be damaged.

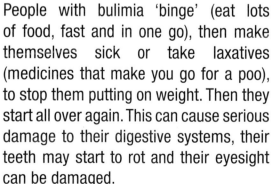

COMPULSIVE EATING

Like bulimia sufferers, compulsive eaters eat large amounts of food in one sitting, even if they're not hungry. But they do not try to get rid of the food. This can make them put on so much weight that they become obese, putting their health seriously at risk.

TOP TIP

Eating disorders are serious illnesses. They can cause long-term health problems, and even death. If you are worried about yourself or a friend, tell an adult you can trust. The sooner you can get proper help, the better your chances of getting better.

PERSONAL HYGIENE

Taking care of your personal hygiene can help you feel better about yourself and boost your positive body image. Here are some top tips:

BODY ODOUR

During puberty, you start to sweat more, especially in your armpits and groin. Everyone sweats sometimes – it helps to cool your body down – but if it mixes with bacteria on your skin, it can start to whiff. This is called BO (body odour). Take a bath or shower every day, and use a deodorant under your arms. Change clothes regularly, especially your underwear.

SKIN CARE

Your skin makes a kind of oil, called sebum, which protects it and keeps it supple and waterproof. The trouble is that puberty can send sebum-production into overdrive. The oil clogs up tiny pores (holes) in your skin and can cause spots. Wash your skin twice a day in warm water, then pat it gently dry. Don't squeeze spots – they'll last longer.

HAIR CARE

You'll probably find that your hair gets greasier, too, and that is also because of sebum. If your hair gets too greasy, you might need to wash it every day. You can also use a shampoo that is specially designed for greasy hair.

HEALTHY TEETH

By the time you're around 14, you will probably have all your adult teeth. They have to last you for life so it pays to take good care of them. Brush your teeth twice a day, for at least two minutes at a time, and have regular check-ups at the dentist. If your teeth grow crooked, you might need braces to straighten them out. This can take some getting used to, but it'll be worth it in the end when you have a beautiful smile!

HEATHY EYES

Take care of your eyes – they are really precious. A healthy diet and exercise can help, as can getting enough sleep. Don't spend too long staring at a screen – this can cause eyestrain. Have regular check-ups at the optician. If you need glasses, there are some super-trendy frames out there, or you may try wearing contact lenses when you're older.

HEALTHY MIND

Having a healthy mind is just as important as having a healthy body. After all, it doesn't matter how healthily you eat or how active you are if you're unhappy, stressed out or constantly worried. The trouble is that growing up can put your brain under serious strain. Powerful hormones whizz around your body, preparing you for becoming an adult. These hormones cause the physical changes in your body but can also cause chaos with your feelings. One minute, you're perfectly happy; the next, you want to scream – it's an emotional roller-coaster, and it can be exciting, frightening and confusing, all at once.

unhappy

stressed

worried

BRAIN STRAIN

All of this is completely normal and nothing to be worried about, though it can feel very alarming at the time. You might find yourself falling out with your friends and family, even though you're not quite sure why. You may find yourself feeling misunderstood or rejected, or simply wanting to be left alone. The good news is that your hormones, and your feelings, will gradually settle down as you get older. In the meantime, understanding what is happening can help you to find ways of coping.

TOP TIP

Remember, you're not alone. Everyone, including your parents, has been through this stage in their lives. Your changing emotions are all part of seeing yourself, and others, in a new and different way. It's not always enjoyable at the time but it won't last for ever.

MOOD SWINGS

Do you sometimes wake up feeling on top of the world but, by evening, feel irritated by everything and everybody? Do your moods and feelings seem to change hour by hour, swinging from happiness to anger in the blink of any eye? Do you suddenly lose your temper over the tiniest thing, without really understanding why? Don't worry – you're not going mad!

As you're finding out, puberty is a tricky time. Stuck between being a child and an adult, you're struggling to find your identity, become more independent and cope with the pressures of school and friends. It's no wonder you're so confused. Your mood swings may well be caused by your hormones and by other changes to your body, which can cause many teenagers to become more self-conscious. You might quarrel with your brothers and sisters, and resent the way that your parents treat you as a child. The ups and downs are hard on everyone, including you.

So, is there anything you can do? Try these tips for taking control of your emotions.

Remember that almost everyone goes through mood swings during puberty.

Get enough sleep – if you're tired, you'll only feel more miserable.

Take up a new sport or activity – it'll make you feel better and take your mind off things.

Do things that make you happy, like dancing around your room.

Wait for your bad mood to pass. If it lasts for too long or feels too much, talk to someone you can trust about how you're feeling.

FACT FLASH

Some girls suffer from mood swings before and during their periods. They may feel grumpy and snappy. This is called premenstrual syndrome or PMS. Gentle exercise, healthy food and plenty of sleep can help to relieve the symptoms, and it will pass when you finish your period. If you feel that it is all a bit too much then ask to see your GP who can help you find some other solutions.

FEELING ANGRY

You may also find yourself feeling angry far more often that you used to. If the slightest thing goes wrong, you explode into a rage. And when you lose your temper, it's really difficult to cool down and think straight again. You just want to be left alone but, somehow, you've got to find a way to get through the day without screaming at your family or friends.

Everyone gets angry sometimes – it's a perfectly normal, healthy emotion. Generally as we grow up we learn to control our anger, but sometimes this can be very tough. The problem comes if your anger makes you act in a way that's harmful to yourself or others. Then you need to try to find out what makes you fly into a rage and learn how to control it. It might be that you think your parents are treating you unfairly. Maybe a kid at school is winding you up. Sometimes, you might not have a clue.

If you do get angry, try not to lose control. Force yourself to count to 10 or breathe deeply until you feel calmer again. However cross you are feeling, it's not okay to hurt other people, break things or make people feel scared.

Ask Dr Christian

I get so angry but I don't know why.

Q. Sometimes I get so angry with my parents I feel like I'm going to explode with rage. It can be over the tiniest thing, but knowing that I'm overreacting doesn't help. What should I do?

A. Controlling your temper can be difficult. Everyone gets angry sometimes - it's a normal emotion, and there's nothing wrong with feeling cross. What really matters is how we handle it. Being angry can make you lose control, get into fights and break things. The first thing is to know when you are feeling angry and why. This is called self-awareness. When you get angry, take a moment to notice what you're feeling and thinking, and this will give you a short time to think about the best way to handle the situation. This self-control helps you not to do things you might regret afterwards, like shouting, swearing and breaking stuff.

It takes time but everyone can learn to control their anger. A good way to start is to think about what you'll gain by doing so. More respect from other people? Less time feeling annoyed and frustrated? A more relaxed approach to life? Walking away from the situation and doing something else for a while can really help. Go for a walk, do some exercise, play a game, listen to some calming music or write down how you are feeling in a diary. Even calling a friend to talk to them about how you feel can help you see the situation in a different way and help diffuse it.

If you feel that your anger is coming too often and is too difficult for you to get under control then ask for help. Anger is a strong emotion and it can feel overwhelming at times. Learning how to deal with it takes effort, practice and patience, but you can do it!

UNDER STRESS

Everyone feels anxious or worried at some time when they're faced with something frightening or stressful. This may be an exam at school or arguments at home. Sometimes these feelings are triggered by upsetting issues in our lives, such as parents' divorce, death of a loved one, being ill or being bullied.

EXAM DAY

Some stress is good for you – it can help you to get things done. But if the stress carries on for a long time it can make you feel ill, and stop you sleeping and eating properly. So, how can you tell if you're suffering from stress?

Are you having trouble sleeping? Do you keep waking up worrying?

Do you feel tense or on edge a lot of the time?

Have you started to avoid situations that make you feel anxious?

Do you find yourself thinking the worst about situations?

Do you find it hard to concentrate?

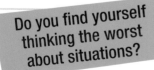

If the answer is yes to any of these, you may be suffering from stress and it could be starting to get in the way of your life.

Try some of these stress-busting tips to make you feel calmer and more in control.

STRESS-BUSTERS

1. Practise deep breathing. Breathe in deeply through your nose for a count of four, breathing from your tummy rather than your chest. Then breathe out slowly through your mouth for a count of eight. Wait a couple of seconds, then do it again.

2. Give yourself a break. If you've got too much going on, talk to your parents about finding something you can drop. It's not a sign of failure, and it doesn't have to be for ever. You can always pick it up again later on.

3. Try to be positive and stop focusing on the bad stuff. Every time you have a negative thought, try to think of a positive one as well.

4. Make a list of all the things that are bothering you. Then try to solve one every two weeks or so. You'll feel better as you cross them off.

5. Keep up the exercise – it's a brilliant stress-buster. It produces hormones that make you feel happier, as well as sleep and eat better.

And if these don't work…

MIND EXERCISE

...try doing some mind exercises instead. Some schools are already trying these as an experiment to see if they can stop teenagers feeling anxious and stressed. Some sessions focus on deep breathing (see page 71). Others include 'thought buses' where you are encouraged to think of your thoughts as buses, and can choose to get on board or let them pass by.

ANGRY

SAD

HAPPY

As you do this, you have to try to focus on the here and now and not think too far ahead. This is called mindfulness. It helps you to stay in the present and not to worry about what may or may not happen in the future. The aim is to help you become more aware of your thoughts and behaviour, and to be able to control them better. If you take time to reflect on negative thoughts that are holding you back, you might be able to think about them in different, more positive ways and become more resilient (able to cope).

FACT FLASH
When you're worried, it can be easy to imagine all sorts of terrible outcomes that are out of proportion to the situation you're in. This is called 'catastrophising' and it can make you feel worse. Concentrating on what's happening now can help you to take better control.

Ask Dr Christian

I hate school and I'm not going back.

Q. I've just started a new school and I'm finding it really hard. I miss all my old friends – I've got no one to talk to here. Plus we've got so much more work to do than last year, and I'm really struggling to keep up. I just feel really overwhelmed.

A. Moving schools is stressful for nearly everyone. And as you get older, I'm afraid that the amount of work that you are given to do will get more and more. Learning how to manage this is a really useful skill to have. One of the most important things is to be as prepared as you can be. Work out what are the most stressful things you are facing, and decide on some ways to make them better. Accept your feelings of stress; they are quite understandable given your situation, and then try to learn all you can about the situation you're dealing with. This might include reading about it, talking to others, or finding out what others in your situation have done and what to expect.

Learning helps you feel more confident and prepared – plus it reminds you that you're not the only one who has gone through this. After you think about your situation and identify and accept the feelings you have, move on to actions you can take to lessen the stress you feel. You could start talking to the person who sits next to you in class and see if you can study together. That could help you make a new friend and catch up on work. Whatever you're facing, it can help to think through the situation, accept the emotions you feel, keep a positive attitude, focus your efforts on what you can influence, get support and care for yourself. All these things can help.

DEPRESSION

As you're growing up it's very common to feel fed up every now and then, but if you've been very sad for several months on end and you're no longer enjoying the things you used to do, you may be suffering from depression. Unlike a bad mood, depression isn't something that you can just snap out of. It's a real illness with real symptoms and you may need to get real help.

Lots of things can cause depression, including stress and difficult times in your life, but it's often a mixture of these. It can feel as if everything is getting on top of you and overwhelming you and that you can't find a way through it. Whatever the cause, you're not alone. People of all ages can become depressed, including children and teenagers.

Depression affects different people in different ways, but if you think that you or one of your friends might be depressed, here are some signs to look out for:

- Feeling sad and hopeless
- Losing interest in your family, friends and the things you used to enjoy
- Losing confidence and feeling worthless
- Finding it hard to concentrate
- Losing motivation to do even small, everyday tasks, or finding them too tough to tackle

If this is happening to you, make sure that you talk to someone – a trusted adult or friend, or your GP. They will have lots of advice for you. Don't be too scared or embarrassed to ask for help. It's not something to be ashamed of. Remember, being depressed isn't your fault. Asking for help doesn't make you a wimp or a weak person. Oh, and you are worth it! Many people feel they don't want to bother their doctor with their problems, but that is EXACTLY what your doctor is there for.

TOP TIP

If you are feeling depressed, it can sometimes help to write things down. Keep a diary and jot down how you are feeling every day. It doesn't matter what you say – no one is going to read it, apart from you.

Ask Dr Christian

I just can't see the point of anything.

Q. Recently I've been feeling really down all the time. I feel quite stressed with school work and I seem to be fighting with my parents a lot, but there's no major drama in my life. I don't want to hang out with my friends any more or do anything. What's wrong with me?

A. Everyone struggles with identity and self-image at your age. You may feel you want to be on your own and make your own decisions, but it can also seem a bit lonely at times and you might often row with family and friends. One important cause for mood swings is biology and your changing hormones. But for some people, and this might apply to you, feeling irritable or short-tempered can be a sign of depression. Many people think of depression as feeling sad, but depression can also bring feelings of moodiness, impatience, anger, or even just not caring. It sounds like you would benefit from talking to someone about how you are feeling. Friends can help each other by realizing that they're not alone in their feelings. Talking to your parents is important, too. Parents can share their own experiences of dealing with bad moods. Plus, they'll appreciate it if you try to explain how you feel instead of just slamming a door! If you are not comfortable talking to your parents just yet, then your favourite teacher or even your GP can help sort through questions about development. Keeping your feelings inside can make them seem much worse, so do try to think of someone you can share with.

Ask Dr Christian

My gran died last week and I can't stop crying.

Q. I'm so sad about my gran passing away. My friends are trying to cheer me up, but I don't feel like going out. I just keep crying all the time. Will this feeling last for ever?

A. Feeling sad because your gran died is perfectly normal. In fact, and it might surprise you to hear this, it is a good thing. Sadness and grief is the reaction you have in response to a death or loss and it can affect you in lots of different ways. You might feel tense, lose your appetite or not be able to concentrate or sleep. You may think a lot about the person who died, and wonder how your life will be without them. You may also feel anger, guilt, despair, relief, love or hope. I think it is really important to feel some of these, and if you need to take some time out by yourself that is fine. Getting over your grief doesn't mean forgetting about the person who has died. Healthy grief is about finding ways to remember loved ones and adjust to life without them present. You might find it helpful to spend some time talking and sharing memories with your family about your gran. It's okay to feel grief for days, weeks or even longer. How intensely you feel grief can be related to things like whether the loss was sudden or expected, or how close you felt to the person who died. Everyone reacts differently and takes a different amount of time to adjust. But as time passes you will start to feel better, cope more easily and remember your gran with happy thoughts rather than just sad ones.

SELF-HARM

Sometimes, teenagers who are feeling very anxious, depressed or bad about themselves hurt or cut themselves deliberately. This is called self-harm. Often it draws blood or leaves a mark, scar or bruise. It can be hard to find out about because people usually do it in secret.

Self-harm is often a cry for help. Many people who self-harm have had unhappy experiences in their lives, which have left them feeling bad about themselves or overwhelmed. The pressure builds up and up, until they feel that hurting themselves is the only way of dealing with it. Sometimes, the physical pain can seem to relieve the way that they are feeling. It can also be a way people have of punishing themselves because they feel worthless.

But self-harming can be very dangerous. Most self-harmers want to stop but don't know how to, or how else to cope with their feelings. If you or someone you know self-harms, talk to someone – there are lots of people out there who can help. You never need to go through it on your own, and the sooner you get help, the sooner you'll get better.

TALKING IT OVER

When you are feeling on top of the world, it's easy to share your good mood with others. But talking about your feelings when you're down can be more difficult. You might feel shy or ashamed to share your problems with someone else. Don't be! Talking about your worries can be really helpful and make problems easier to cope with. It can help you to work out a way of dealing with things, or can help simply by getting them out in the open.

Choosing the right person to talk with is important. You might have a best friend who you share everything with, and that's great. But make sure your friends are trustworthy and won't break your confidence. For some things, an older brother or sister or your parents might be a better choice. It may feel strange telling them your worries, but keep going – they will try their best to help you. If you can't open up to them completely, or you're not sure that they'll understand, talk to another trusted adult, such as a teacher, your GP or another health professional. What you tell them will be confidential so you can be as honest and open as you like.

TOP TIP

If you prefer it, there are plenty of helplines you can call (see pages 92–93). You can speak to someone anonymously (you don't need to give your name). This may be easier for you as you can be sure that they won't judge you or tell anyone else.

Ask Dr Christian

My friend needs help...

Q. My friend confided in me that she's been self-harming, but swore me to secrecy. I'm really worried about her and I don't know how to help. Should I tell someone?

A. Your friend is obviously having a difficult time and knows that cutting herself is not the best thing to be doing. I think the fact that she has told you means that she wants some help, but doesn't know who to ask or is worried that she'll get into trouble. It can be very difficult to know how to help but there are people, like a therapist or counsellor, who are better able to help people cope with life's struggles. Getting professional help to overcome the problem doesn't mean that someone is weak or crazy. Therapists and counsellors are trained to help people discover inner strengths that help them heal. These inner strengths can then be used to cope with life's problems in a healthy way. Your school may have a student counsellor or nurse and I think they will be the best person for you to talk to about how to help your friend.

Ask Dr Christian

How can I feel more positive?

Q. I always seem to focus on the worst possible outcomes, and sometimes it stops me from even trying things in case I fail. Just before exams last year I was so convinced I wouldn't pass that I didn't bother revising that hard. What can I do to be more positive?

A. Thinking positively about yourself and about what you are doing really can make a difference to how well you do things. Research shows that people feel and do their best when they experience at least three times as many positive emotions as negative ones. So how can you help to boost your positive thoughts? Think about the positive emotions you are already familiar with, and think about which activities, situations or people are involved when you tend to feel each emotion. This will help you to be more aware of the positive feelings you already experience, and the situations or activities that bring them. Then, if you want to feel those positive emotions again, sometimes it's as simple as thinking about those people, or going off and doing those activities for a bit. Listening to a song, making a phone call or playing with your pet can all make a big difference. Why not agree to do this several times a day to boost your positive thoughts? As you work on increasing your positive emotions, you might notice that you feel happier, more accomplished and more energetic. A small daily investment of focusing on the positive pays off with big lifetime rewards.

HEALTHY FUTURE

If you eat healthily and stay active while you're young, you'll see the benefits for the rest of your life. You might wonder 'why bother with all that stuff?' You feel fine as you are and besides, you can always start tomorrow. The rest of your life probably seems a very long way away. But, get into good habits now and you'll stand a much better chance of staying healthy and feeling better as you get older. That's a fact!

It's also well known that a balanced diet and exercise can help you fight off common illnesses, such as coughs and colds. You'll probably still catch them, but you'll be able to get rid of them more quickly. You'll also feel less tired, less stressed and generally better able to cope with your hectic lifestyle and the growing pains of puberty. And finally, feeling healthy will help you to feel happier – what's not to like about that?

WHAT IS OBESITY?

Obesity means that someone is so overweight that it is likely to damage their health. With our generally less active lifestyles, obesity is becoming a big problem in our society, both for children and adults. This is because it causes lots of health problems, both now and in the future.

If you are obese, you are more likely to suffer from illnesses, such as high blood pressure, heart disease and type 2 diabetes at some point in your life. Obese people are also more likely to have asthma, arthritis and to become depressed. Some cancers are also thought to be linked to obesity. In short, being obese can impact a person's whole life. The longer you have a problem with your weight for, the harder and harder it is to do something about it. Sort out your diet and exercise routine while you are young and weight doesn't have to be an issue for the rest of your life.

People may become obese if they eat more food than their bodies need, and store the extra calories as fat. They may eat a lot of food that isn't good for them, not do enough exercise or have other problems. Some people have genes which make them more likely to become obese. Whatever the reason, a healthy diet and staying active can help people to lose weight. You don't need to do it all at once. Aim to cut down any unhealthy and junk food gradually and, at the same time, start eating more of the right things. Let yourself have treats sometimes, and make healthy choices where you can. You'll soon find that the healthier you eat, the healthier you feel and you'll be setting up good habits for life.

TOP TIP

Sometimes, people eat too much because they are bored or unhappy. They use food as a way of coping with their feelings. The trouble is that once the food is gone, the feelings are still there. Try to work out which feelings trigger your eating. Then use this to make better choices. If you're bored, for example, phone a friend rather than reaching for the ice cream.

Ask Dr Christian

Am I allergic to bread?

Q. Sometimes I feel bloated or get a tummy ache if I eat lots of bread. I've read about coeliac disease – could I have that? Should I stop eating all wheat?

A. There are lots and lots of different possible causes for the way you sometimes feel, including simply eating too much! Suddenly cutting out whole groups of food can lead to all sorts of health problems, and means that your diet will not be as balanced as it should be. You will probably read a lot about people cutting out foods for various reasons but I would never recommend you do this without talking to a doctor first. If you think you are having problems then ask someone to book you an appointment with your GP. Many people say that they have intolerances to foods, but very few of those people actually do.

Ask Dr Christian

My friend is trying to make me smoke.

Q. Some of the girls at school have started smoking because they say it helps you lose weight. Is that true? They've been pushing me to smoke too and say I'm babyish if I don't want to. What can I do?

A. Having people try to persuade you to do something that you don't really want to do is very common in life, and it is really useful to learn how to manage it. The pressure to do what others are doing can be powerful and hard to resist and may make you do something that has serious consequences. Giving in to the pressure to dress a certain way is one thing, going along with the crowd to drink or smoke is another. Using alcohol or smoking increases your chances of giving in to peer pressure on other things, like drugs. Substance use impairs judgement and interferes with your ability to make good decisions. So smoking, for many reasons, is definitely something you should say no to. It can make you feel very sick, make you very ill, and even can make you die young. Listen to your gut feeling: if you feel uncomfortable, even if your friends seem to be okay with what's going on, it means that something about the situation is wrong for you and you should walk away. Doing this will make you a leader, not a follower.

SCREEN TIME

With so much technology at your fingertips, you most likely spend hours each week or even every day staring at a screen. Keeping up with your friends, learning new things and playing computer games is fun, but spending too much time on your phone or computer can be a real pain. Staring at a screen can be tough on your body, especially your hands and eyes. Here's why, plus some tips about what you do about it...

RSI (REPETITIVE STRAIN INJURY) – pain in your hands, wrists, arms, neck and shoulders caused by doing something (like typing) for a long time, without a rest. Make sure that you sit properly when you're typing with your fingers and wrists level with your forearms, and take plenty of breaks. When you're sending texts, use all of your fingers, not just your thumbs.

EYE STRAIN – any time that you're staring at a screen, your eyes are hard at work. Too much screen time can put them under serious strain. Make sure that your screen is at eye level, and keep taking plenty of breaks. Focus your eyes on something else by looking out of the window to give them a well-earned rest.

BACK ACHE – it's important to sit properly in a chair, with your bottom back in the seat and your back touching the seat back all the time. Try not to slouch or lean over your keyboard (this also applies when you're writing). Support your feet on a footrest or pile of books. If you are tall for your age then back ache can be more of a problem – it was for me. Doing some exercises to strengthen your lower back and tummy muscles can really help.

TOP TIP

Ideally, you should limit your screen time to no more than two hours a day. It's not a good idea to sit at your computer for more than 30 minutes at a time, without taking a break, so keep getting up, moving about and doing something else!

AND THAT'S IT...

Wow! Well that's about it I think. We have covered loads of important stuff and I really hope you now feel more confident and more in control of growing up. I know that some things will still throw you, upset you or baffle you, but if you use what you have learned here then I am quite sure you will cope. Remember, just take some time out, breathe and think before you act. And if you're not sure, then just ask. Someone will always have been there before you, and will know what to do. One day maybe you will write a book about your experiences growing up, and give others tips and advice too. After all, that's what I did!

Dr Christian

RESOURCES

UK SITES:

NHS CHOICES
Tips on healthy living for everyone, covering a huge range of topics.
http://www.nhs.uk/livewell/Pages/Livewellhub.aspx

Healthy eating:
http://www.nhs.uk/Livewell/Goodfood/Pages/healthy-eating-teens.aspx

Sleep tips:
http://www.nhs.uk/Livewell/Childrenssleep/Pages/teensleeptips.aspx

Mental health:
http://www.nhs.uk/livewell/youth-mental-health/pages/Youth-mental-health-help.aspx

NHS Change 4 Life
Advice on becoming healthier and happier.
http://www.nhs.uk/change4life/Pages/change-for-life.aspx

FOOD - A FACT OF LIFE
A wealth of free resources about healthy eating, cooking, food and farming for children and young people aged 3 to 18 years.
www.foodafactoflife.org.uk

GREAT ORMOND STREET HOSPITAL: STAYING HEALTHY

Advice for teenagers about staying healthy, produced by the experts at Great Ormond Street Hospital (GOSH). It's packed with top tips to help you lead a more active and healthy lifestyle as you grow up into an adult.
http://www.gosh.nhs.uk/teenagers/ staying-healthy

BBC RADIO 1 ADVICE

BBC Advice factfiles are here to help young people with a broad range of issues. Helping you get through life with the straight facts on your issues.
www.bbc.co.uk/radio1/advice

CHILDLINE

ChildLine is a private and confidential service for children and young people up to the age of 19. You can contact a ChildLine counsellor about anything – no problem is too big or too small.
http://www.childline.org.uk/

US SITES:

TEEN HEALTH

A safe, private place for teens who need honest, accurate information and advice about health, emotions and life.
http://kidshealth.org/teen/

GIRLS HEALTH

Girlshealth.gov offers girls reliable, useful information on health and well-being. Their tagline is "Be Happy. Be Healthy. Be You. Beautiful." It focuses on the idea that being yourself – finding what makes you smile and how to live well – is what makes you "you." And that is beautiful!
http://www.girlshealth.gov/

INDEX